Nowhere Near Morning

Poems by

Jeffrey M. Bernstein

Liquid Light Press

Premium Chapbook First Edition

Copyright © 2013 by Jeffrey M. Bernstein

ISBN-10: 098830726X

ISBN-13: 978-0-9883072-6-1

Liquid Light Press

poetry that speaks to the heart

www.liquidlightpress.com

Cover Art & Design by Clay Rodery
Cover Design by M. D. Friedman
(*www.mdfriedman.com*)
Photo of Poet by Stacey Cushner
Photo of Cisco by Ally Bernstein

Contents

The Voices In My Head 1

Last Rites 3

Under the Daybed 5

Architecture Lessons 7

Oblivion Is Also the Name 8

Transformations 10

What I'll Never Learn 12

Cisco 13

Entering Vermont 14

A Few Days After They Let Me Leave the Hospital 22

Elegy or Ode 24

Photo On My Desk 26

Where Do Dowagers Go When the Last Timbers Fall? 27

Sashaying Through Connecticut 29

Press Release from the Governor 31

You've Reached Dr. Freud's Answering Service 32

About the Author 37

Credits and Acknowledgements 37

For Stacey, Ben and Ally. You are my all.

The Voices In My Head

What did I hear
when my left ear
shut down, punctured
drum leaving me
first with faint sounds
like when you put
a seashell
to your head?

Even a perfect conch
or whelk on Florida
beach doesn't get
that many frequencies.
I think I heard small
children playing about
one hundred years
ago. Occasionally,

old time transistor
radio static made
an appearance, tinny reception
hard to pin down. Even
post-war crystal radio showed
up — just one station,
no 100,000 watts
of pow, pow, power.

I heard the ballgame broadcast,
lost in pre-steroids days
when a guy played his whole
career for just one
team. Then people started
to whisper. I think I might
know who they were
but can't be sure.

Last Rites

Trips to the cancer clinic have the same rhythm
each time, except that he gets weaker.
Still we are sustained by
that father-firstborn bond.

He tells me I look worried. *You think?*
I ask. The chill air in my car (he doesn't
even have the strength to utter his usual
*turn off the air-conditioning and you'll save
some gas*) gives way to the blast furnace
of a parking garage as we cross to the elevator,
descend into the bowels of that special hospital,
pass Ted Williams and Green Monster
on the wall, heading for that awful beam,
the best they can muster.

The Jamaicaway Oaks spell July.
I don't want to be there.

What could he have been thinking?
Which places was he visiting in that grim
perfect cellar? Palliative, strange word,
comes from the Latin, to cloak.
Yet it also means to relieve the suffering.
Which is it? To ease or to hide?

Some of us would rather know
the truth. My father did. That way
when the doorbell rings there's no surprise.
He had everything ready to go.

Under the Daybed

are several boxes full of prescription pads,
off-white vellum slips that advertise
this pharmaceutical company-- that healthcare
conglomerate -- why my last name's at the top
in bold letters! I usually faint at the sight of blood --
never took a science class after tenth grade.
I find myself studying those scripts
on an evening when the light hangs around
like teenagers on a pre-digital, pre-video corner;
return to them when winter nights seep
the breakwater beyond that brackish
coastal pond of our liquid planet.

There are several vintages: the oldest date themselves
-- four numbers led by a neighborhood
and exchange like "Longwood 6"
for the white coat crowd.
Now, even area codes tell nothing.
I've never actually written a single
prescription, just thought about doing it
for years since the call came to pack up
father's office after first Labor Day
following his death. I took a few coffee mugs
that I still use five years later; diplomas
and medical accoutrements went to my sister
the neurologist and little brother got the knick-knacks.

I was the only one who wanted those boxes,
couldn't see parting with those talismans.
I'd no sooner toss the hundreds of books
he'd bought over the years, alphabetized
on shelf after shelf of his apartment
overlooking the river.

I imagine the DEA knocking at my front door
one of these days. Course, they don't know
about Emerson-like advice that I deliver
instead, humor being the best
possible medicine I am licensed to dispense.
Sometimes, the recipients listen, wait
for the salves to course like waves
on long nights along some tropical beach,
Marley singing not to worry about a thing,
believe it for a little while.

Architecture Lessons

Rarely is an arch of an eyebrow
a signal achievement, but the other night
I drove south to visit my children at school,
show them how the right side of my face
refused to obey, right eyebrow
a flag stuck at half mast, brow half-smooth
no matter how hard I grimaced, crooked
smile to boot, all courtesy
of mysterious palsy, modern medicine
stuck in nineteenth century when some
Scottish surgeon discovered a condition
for which he could not figure out the cause.

Son and daughter fidgeted in their seats,
they already knew enough.

Oblivion Is Also the Name

of a trail, white gash
on a high shoulder
of Mt. Tecumseh, skier's right.

At age eight, my son flew
off the icy lip, disappeared
over a cliff while brightly

colored skiers flashed
above like tropical fish
unaware of sharks

beyond the reef. Zeus took pity
and gave me strength
to clamber down

to retrieve my boy
from precarious perch
holding tightly to an ash,

slightly stunned, teary,
goggles broken, flag-
starred racing helmet

the thin thread
between darkness
and our fortunate lives.

Was my heart beating harder
than his? How many times
each day do we near

those threads, slight
as the lightest monofilament
that even the fish cannot see?

Transformations

At four, a simple children's book so terrified
my son that next night he screamed for me
to come into his room. "How do I know
you aren't an aardvark?" he asked
when I opened his door. "I don't think
you are my Dad." I lawyered
high and low, employed every strategy
Dr. Spock recommended, presented
the law and facts on my side, threw
in a few I invented on the spot.

"How do you think an aardvark could get
all the way here from Africa?" I sat next
to him on the bed, felt him settle a bit,
dig under the covers. "Could he figure out how
to get to the airport in Johannesburg, come up
with the cash to buy a plane ticket all the way
to Boston (it costs more money than you have
ever seen)." I put my hand on his back,
could feel his breathing become more regular.

"And then how would he find the right bus
to the Blue Line, pop in a subway token,
change upstairs at Government Center
and take the Riverside train all the way
to Waban Station?" He was heading off
but I couldn't resist closing arguments.
"And besides, I'd clobber him at the front door,
the dog would bark, he'd never get in.
Yup, I am your Dad, no worries."

The only real shape-shifters are dead
or got pretty damn near close. I know
for certain *my* Dad's usually a Barred Owl,
sometimes a hawk, once an ant bearing a leaf
that traced the raised gold "BERNSTEIN"
on the warm, summer-grassed gravestone.

Now I can see that lone coyote at meadow's edge
as clearly as if I were standing next to him,
can make out the tidal waves speeding in
from the Atlantic, can get that broken key
to start up your car as if I were the engine.
I only change shape when everyone else
is sleeping, save the dogs.

What I'll Never Learn

I'd like to know almost every detail of that solo trip east across America, just what my daughter was thinking as she crossed the Great Plains, wind turbines decorating the horizon for tens of miles. Was she looking for dry storms that lit the high desert like fireworks? Lost inside her own thoughts or in the places passing by? She spent days speeding through EZPass gates that framed the Midwest like rooms in that open-walled dollhouse I assembled for her when she was five. I don't want to hear though about the gas station in the sketchy neighborhood leaving Cleveland, men hanging near the pumps leering at her Utah-tanned legs. She did call me a few hundred miles west of Vermont to report that it was raining. She'd forgotten how much she loved gray skies and hadn't seen the clouds open up like that in months.

I would like to listen to any story my son cares to tell of playing music in clubs in Detroit, Nashville and a baker's dozen or so other venues across Mid-America and South, shots after the show with the home-band. Were there dark-eyed girls hanging on his every word, inviting him to crash? They must have studied him standing behind his electric keyboard, leaning into those keys, red beard shining in the lights like a lighthouse far off in the fog. Oh, he told me a bit about the barbeque at some riverside outdoor club in Asheville and there were always texts punctuating the days to let us know how much steamy ground they'd covered. But mostly I imagined all of those hours in the van with the band passing the overpasses covered with kudzu.

If I ask, I'll never find out. Details will leak out when you least expect it, tiny flowers bloom in between the bricks, runners really, years after you planted the primary specimens.

Cisco

The dead are the lucky ones in that Utah town, cast-off, as it is, in the tumbleweeds among the prairie dogs and rotted highway U.S. 6, high desert. The twenty or so residents? None too friendly to lookie-loos who stop by the old general store, the gas station and the rusted trailers that once passed for home. The wind rattles the few shingles remaining on the tar-paper shacks. The living don't want us here, feel they speak for the ghosts, but those ghouls don't give a fig what we do, inspect, where we walk. Still the air feels close, which is strange, given the lively wind among the departed.

Saturday morning, the next-to-last day I'll see my daughter for I don't know how long. She ventures into a broken-down building and I feel that sharp pang that I try to repress before it's too late. And once the plane pulls up, my words get lost in the desert.

Oh, you can put up a firebreak or three but that only gives the illusion of comfort, can't stop the dry winds that drive those spring flames across the roads, burn decades-old skeletons while the living only shout and swear.

Entering Vermont

You'll wait a long, long time for anything much
To happen in heaven beyond the floats of cloud
And the Northern Lights that run like tingling nerves.
The sun and moon get crossed, but they never touch,
Nor strike out fire from each other, nor crash out loud.
The planets seem to interfere in their curves
But nothing ever happens, no harm is done
We may as well go patiently on with our life
And look elsewhere than to stars and moon and sun
For the shocks and changes we need to keep us sane.

From "On Looking Up by Chance at the Constellations"
by Robert Frost

On your first night back, children play hide and seek
and flashlight tag under those big old oaks across the way.

You fall asleep and dream of the three gold Cross pens
from that long-gone stationery store outside Harvard Square,

gifts from your father over the decades, you'd
lost them all and found them over and over again.

Next morning, sit on the brick steps, watch a bird
glide a short distance, you've never seen flying before!

Those same nineteenth century oaks beckon
as they stretch for the suburban sky, verdant twist.

Last week, your son asked why you made
the choices you did. Next morning answers:

five a.m. cue thunder and lightning;
six a.m. tap screensaver, bright sun

appearing in that high window
where you'd watched tall branches tremble.

Why does a closed-loop suddenly open,
almost fail, and seal again?

Every rustle in the leaves is another invasion.
You've had your share of needles lately

stopped watching the lines running in and out.
The gales rise and fall like irregular heartbeats

but you're still here, can think about the dark
only so long until you wander off

on one of those bike paths kids carved
along the old aqueduct. Decades past,

you skimmed those same trails on skis
when city plows ignored the cross-streets

and it used to snow a lot. You could go
for miles and forget where you were.

The mounds and dips are more gradual now,
accreting over time like plaque in our arteries.

It is hard to know where to start
but you keep seeing your father's hand

on a baseball ready to throw a curve,
sphere so white, sharp stitches blood red.

It came to you after he died that his favorite
part of taking you to Fenway was that

you'd let his pitching hand rest on your shoulder,
even as an easily embarrassed teenager

you didn't complain about that slight touch.
After-dinner deadheading petunias

slows your breath better than any medication.
They measure heartbeats and blood pressure,

why not the sound of trees growing, the oxygen
that pours out of the forest, the rise and fall

of your chest, now there's a sweet blanket
as the first curtains of rain slice Route 12?

You can see behind it, on the other side there's
not a drop, as dry as the best incision. You've passed

by, emerged from between those high granite walls,
constantly scanning the horizon for a slash of light.

You don't know anything, you know *everything*.
Part of you is invincible now.

You wake again and again at 4 a.m., look
for your youngest - it's always that Tuesday

when you staggered against the sink
in hospital bathroom, only two days had passed

since your goodbye at Logan as she boarded
her first flight for eight thousand mile journey

to Taiwan, you could not have pictured
yourself in some ER, you thought

that she would never get to say goodbye,
you wondered what the rest of her life

would be like without you. But come morning
there you are, dogs sleeping at your side.

Steamy air feels good, the late afternoon
breezes feel better. A car slips by silently,

must be electric, the road some old-fashioned
mail chute, with air whooshing everything along.

Each tree is a separate woodblock;
why they make you wonder where you learned

to tell your children that you loved them
more than the universe, you don't know.

We think we understand the construct, forget
that our planet is mostly green and blue:

the blood coursing the passages never
felt better and everywhere that canopy!

Ocean was slate-angry that day your son took
you across Brooklyn to Coney Island;

your teeth were sand-whipped along the deserted
boardwalk: you waited, brooded, worried.

You've shown him how to worry
if nothing else and you imagine your son

studying the instruments over the hospital bed,
sight-reading like the musician he is,

agonizing, that image is too hot.
Instead, feel summer's first sweet corn,

undulant stalks waving you down
the cracked state road.

You find yourself sitting oh so close
to your flaxen-haired wife on a warm stone wall

overlooking a medieval cathedral
in some Provencal hill town

one late afternoon, the village is deserted
save you two. There is no need to talk.

Meditate until 5 p.m. and Isabelle wakes you,
puts her chocolate head on your chest

to remind you that it is dinnertime,
fixes her eyes as if to say

you have exactly fifteen minutes.
In March, somewhere in Iowa or Nebraska

your daughter said *you are deep
green and I am dark. Deep greens*

*are optimists who know we've fucked up
our planet but still think it isn't too late*

*and technology can solve it. Dark greens know
it is but still you do what you can.*

So you work in your little corner, cope
with searing summers way up north,

hurricanes which visit locales
that you had guaranteed her were havens.

She hasn't yet realized she's as deep
as the afternoon shadows on a Vermont hillside,

the rough passages still too present as the plains
recede at 75 m.p.h. in the rearview mirror,

music coaxing us through the monotony
of arrow-straight highways until

the first ranges of the Rockies grow
on the horizon like some wondrous crop.

What do we know for certain?
Maybe you should listen to all the songs

on your iTunes playlist. It will take 19.5 days
but what's the hurry?

Yesterday the thunder and lightning circled the meadow
as if at the center of some vast amphitheater

but the rains never came. This afternoon, you can feel it
building, know it's coming. It will sweep the valley,

fill the Gulf Stream, slicken storm-wracked macadam,
carry August towards fall, the darkness,

break the heat, herald those Canadian breezes.
Life is a long text message, blue iPhone bubbles

natter, chatter across the world, the wind
in the upper branches sounds like water

as it rushes past your life's high tideline
and everywhere cicadas say *summer is over*.

Pandora starts to play oldies (nothing
like the channel you selected). Steely Dan,

Van Morrison and The Band fill the room
as you write. Disobedience has you singing along.

Remember when you opened those varnished walnut
cabinets, played Cat Stevens on the downstairs stereo,

and Dad said *turn that down* and you wouldn't
and punishment was a portable stereo for your room?

I could see him trying hard not to smile. I do the same
thing with my kids, channel him every time.

A lot of mornings you are up way before anyone else.
Sometimes you cry for yourself, but mostly for your daughter.

If the dogs are in the room they ask to go outside.
Go back to sleep, you say, *it's nowhere near morning*.

A Few Days After They Let Me Leave the Hospital

I found myself in overgrown grass
studying the raised lettering on the horizontal
stone, Jewish star, all those sevens.
It was exactly five years after father's last
witching hour. I thought about how close
I had gotten to joining him; my sister, brother
and I drank a bit of Glenlivet, his favorite,
in the paper cups I'd brought along for the occasion.
I always scan the sky for signs when I visit
but siblings only looked down, sipped scotch,
missed entirely the huge Red-tailed Hawk
perched in the tree to the south. Buteo pulled
his wingspan in tight, then sat motionless,
surveying our doings: the poems we read,
the scotch we sprinkled on the grave,
the pot of red flowers.

"There's Dad," I said, but sister and brother
did not believe me. I knew better though.
I am the oldest and tattooed now
by the days in the ICU when only half
of my blood could be accounted for,
watching heart monitors and whatnot
through my own morphine haze. I thought

how much he loved this life, hung on every

word we'd each tell him about our lives,

welcomed each month faithfully with a *Rabbit, Rabbit*

before he got out of bed, worried about

us so hard you could feel it hundreds

of miles away. I inhaled a perfect breeze

for dinner, thanked everyone in sight

for staying on this side. I remembered

the scorching heat at his funeral,

knew again it was not yet time, not yet time.

Elegy or Ode

Great Uncle Jack ("Jeck" to my grandfather)
had named his sleek yacht "Elysium."
I boarded it just once, summer 1964, slept
overnight in an elegant wood-paneled cabin
and after a breakfast of toast and jam
at a pop-up table in the stern
was fitted out with an orange life preserver
jumped off with my cousins
into the dark, dark water
of the outer harbor.
Floating a few yards away, that vessel
looked like the White House
did to tourists gazing from the iron fence
at 1600 Pennsylvania Avenue. (I'd seen
the real one for my first time
one week after November 22, 1963.)
I thought about what might be
swimming below me in the dark
gray-blue water of the outer harbor
dead-eyed sharks, wanted to be back
on that boat, back on the pier
back in my own landlocked bed
as soon as humanly possible.

A well-meaning "friend" wrote
to tell me that my July "NDE"
would be the very best thing
that ever happened to me.
I doubt he's had a similar experience.
I didn't ask to bleed like that.
Had no idea it was coming.
It populates waking dreams at 3 or 4 a.m.
My eyes are sleepy all the time
my reading glasses might need a boost
but I can see deep into the woods
even after the light fades.

Photo On My Desk

My brother kneels over, pats
the original chocolate labrador
on the deck of the Vineyard ferry -
could it be the old Naushon?
The sky is mostly blue though
there are white mountains

on the watery horizon. I used to think
endless summer was inside
that frame but the brown dog is long
gone, my brother's older, I am older still.
But it's about the photographer,
his hand as subtle as the shift
in the breeze
just beyond the wake.

Where Do Dowagers Go When the Last Timbers Fall?

Trees have claimed that spot
where the Soo-Nipi Lodge stood,
a few minutes' walk from the one
sandy beach on the lake.

When I was a child it was a haunted mansion,
timbers collapsed on the front porch, door
frames listing to port -- or was it starboard?
Windows sagged, shattered glass decorated
hedges, the only upright soldiers turrets
and garrets. ("Stand up straight," mother'd say.)

Now its name has been stolen
for some Olde New England "concept"
whose only visitors are granite-
countered, stone-chimneyed houses
that say "hey sailor, wanna get some
'gracious living' by the lake?"

I remember Thursday nights
waiting, waiting, waiting
on the fence in front of the Lodge;
August deepened, and so did the darkness.
I no longer needed to listen
for the sound of father's tires
on the gravel, but scanned instead
for the play of headlights on the birches.

Is life like that as we age? As night
nears, don't search for shadows –
just feel the solids become liquid,
water turns to gas, all softly aglow.

Sashaying Through Connecticut

Saturday night on the Amtrak local
to Boston – they call it regional
but it seems pretty poky where I sit –
listening to podcast of Irish writer
read John Cheever's "The Swimmer":

He needed a drink. Whiskey would warm him,
pick him up, carry him through the last
of his journey, refresh his feeling
that it was original and valorous
to swim across the county...

I am oh so rudely interrupted when
two passengers fail to disembark
at Bridgeport, they bitch and moan,
forced to ride all the way to New Haven.

At crossings along the coastline,
red lights blink in barely spring mist
like sparring spouses – is it last call
or not? I watch cars ease out
from parking lots of taverns and bars
in Old Saybrook, Mystic, no name
towns. They seem to wobble,
pause as we trundle by.

Cheever says we're all drinkers,
there's a sting in the beast's tail
you don't know what
it is until it is too late.

Press Release from the Governor

Montpelier. They say the last mile of Irene-cracked road will reopen today at 3 p.m. You wouldn't want to cut a ribbon under the circumstances, better to retie it or weave some subtle tapestry of winter color, conifer green, maple brown, road ash. Yearning for the northern lights, we all yearn for something. When they take away something that was there your whole life the loss won't process at first. You keep looking around the corner, think you see it but it's nothing but vapors, snow-mist. Eventually the gray matter fills the void; the color isn't there — that limb a twitchy memory.

You've Reached Dr. Freud's Answering Service

I'm not sure why I drove all that way
to take a ferry back and forth across the Sound,
but dreams don't always make sense.

Might be they hold great insights
you'd get no other way but
to summon them from nether regions
of the blanket, they may have fallen
clear to the floor or slipped behind
the headboard, hunting dustbunnies.

Once recalled you can try to interpret dreams
but take a literal approach
and it might just be your cortex
taking out the garbage, no recycling them
in those snazzy green barrels
for which the city charges fifty bucks apiece.
Or maybe just toss them out like
old-fashioned trash but now they belong
in those cobalt blue receptacles —
pay as you throw!

You could try to keep paper and pen
by your bedside, wake anyone
who happens to be sharing the mattress
(the dogs snore on) when a new one pops
like a wet spot in that log on the fire.
Next morning your scrawl
would be indecipherable,
like reading a language
with no written form.

When people claim they had a dreamless sleep,
they enter the interstate at seventy mph
in some rural burg, wake up in the suburbs
and wonder how they got there. You know,
like those travelers on New Year's Eve
who head south on the divided
highway's northbound lanes
and morning never comes,
just that pale light
when the sun should be ready to rise.

About the Author

A lifelong New Englander, Jeff Bernstein divides his time between Boston and Central Vermont. Except on summer days when his beloved Red Sox are at Fenway, he prefers to rattle along back roads, although he is proud to be a Bostonian. Poetry is his favorite and earliest art form. (He can't draw a whit or hold a tune.) Recent poems have appeared or are forthcoming in *Ballard Street Poetry Journal, Birchsong — A Poetry Anthology (Blueline Press), Best Indie Lit New England, Loch Raven Review, Main Street Rag, Muddy River Poetry Review, Paper Nautilus, Reckless Writing Poetry Anthology, San Pedro River Review* and *Tipton Poetry Review.* His first chapbook, *Interior Music,* was published in 2010 by Foothills Publishing. Jeff's writer's blog is *www.hurricanelodge.com.*

Credits and Acknowledgements

Poems in this chapbook previously appeared in the following publications:

"Architecture Lessons," *Ballard Street Poetry Journal*
"Last Rites," *The Stray Branch*
"Oblivion Is Also the Name," *Loch Raven Review*
"Elegy or Ode," *Muddy River Poetry Review*

Other Books by Jeffrey M. Bernstein

Interior Music (Foothills Publishing, Kanona, NY, 2010)

Other Books from Liquid Light Press

All Liquid Light Press books are available directly from *liquidlightpress.com* or from any of the current major global distribution channels including Amazon, Barnes and Noble, the iBookstore and the Ingram Catalog.

Leaning Toward Whole, **Poems by M. D. Friedman (Released June, 2011)**
This poetry chapbook from the international award winning poet, M. D. Friedman, contains pieces both poignant and personal. It speaks to both the universal and the everyday, both the moment and the millennium.

The Miracle Already Happening - Everyday Life with Rumi, **Poems by Rosemerry Wahtola Trommer (Released December, 2011)**
Rosemerry Wahtola Trommer's superb collection of poems, inspired by Rumi, is full of heart, humor, peace and wisdom. This chapbook gracefully flings us from our routine into the joy of life, bristles with surprise and dances with mystic vision.

Spiral, **Poems by Lynda La Rocca (Released March, 2012)**
Award winning poet, Lynda La Rocca, creates a compelling poetic and melodic discourse from the persistent cravings and fears inside of each of us. This book is both as darkly sweet and satisfying as chocolate and as nourishing and healing as mother's chicken soup.

From the Ashes, **Poems by Wayne A. Gilbert (Released June , 2012)**
Master jazz Sufi poet, Wayne A. Gilbert, chronicles the loss of his mother with powerful, bittersweet honesty to create this beautiful collection of poems that is universal in its scope, transcendent in the depth of its understanding and exquisitely musical in form.

ah, **Poems by Rachel Kellum (Released July, 2012)**
Rachel Kellum's *ah* is a transparent poetic odyssey into the ethereal that is both provocative and inspirational. Rachel Kellum demonstrates a maturity of craft that bespeaks the power of poetry to suggest what logic always struggles to explain about our divine nature.

Catalyst, **Poems by Jeremy Martin (Released December, 2012)**
Jeremy Martin's *Catalyst* is a mind field of delight. It explodes with incendiary insight, cosmic playfulness and dizzying joy. It lifts us up on the back of a rocket and leaves in the weightless orbit of inner self.

Of Eyes and Iris, **Poems by Erika Moss Gordon (Released March, 2013)**
Erica Moss Gordon's *Of Eyes and Iris* shines with the purity of a mountain stream, dances with sunlight, and shivers with the chill of perception. Refreshing with its simplicity yet rich in wisdom, her poetry punctuates its quite voice with echoes of illumination.

Your House Is Floating, **Poems by Susan Whitmore (Released June, 2013)**
Susan Whitmore's craft is as smooth and crisp as olive oil on fresh garden greens. The body of her poetry hums with the efficiency of a long distant runner, and the soul of her words is as electric and warm as the colors of sunset. The shadow cast by her images glow with enduring light.